The Science of Passionate Interests

The Science of Passionate Interests:

An Introduction to Gabriel Tarde's Economic Anthropology

Bruno Latour and Vincent Antonin Lépinay

PRICKLY PARADIGM PRESS
CHICAGO

Prickly Paradigm Press, LLC
5629 South University Avenue
Chicago, Il 60637

www.prickly-paradigm.com

ISBN-10: 0-9794057-7-7
ISBN-13: 978-0-979-4057-7-8
LCCN: 2009936907

Printed in the United States of America on acid-free paper.

The tendency to *mathematize* economic science and the tendency to *psychologize* it, far from being irreconcilable, should rather, in our view, lend each other mutual support.

The doctrine of laissez-faire therefore has the greatest affinity with that of society-as-organism, and the blows aimed at the former rebound on the latter.
—Gabriel Tarde*

Imagine how things might have turned out had no one ever paid attention to *Das Kapital*. A century later, the book would have been rediscovered and people would have been struck with amazement by its scope and audacity—an isolated, little understood work, without any scientific, political or social impact; a work that had generated neither disciples nor exegeses, and one that no attempts at application had come to transform. How different the history of the 20th century would have been had the bible of men of action been Gabriel Tarde's *Psychologie Économique*, published in 1902, instead of Marx's work! But perhaps it is not too late to reinvent, through a little essay in historical fiction, a

---

*All references to the 1902 manuscript of *Psychologie Économique* are accessible online via the Prickly Paradigm website (www.prickly-paradigm.com/catalog.html). In that version, all page numbers are from the original version of *Psychologie Économique* as it appears on Gallica, the *Bibliotheque Nationale de France* website (http://gallica.bnf.fr).

theory of political economy in which Tarde plays the role that, in the real course of history, was occupied by Marx.

At first glance, it seems difficult to take seriously the ramblings of this sociologist who had no disciples; who treats conversation among idlers as a "factor of production"; who denies the central role attributed to poor old labor; who distinguishes, in the notion of capital, the "seed" or "germ" (the *software*) from the "cotyledon" (the *hardware*), to the advantage of the former; who follows, with equal attentiveness, fluctuations in the price of bread and variations in the prestige of political figures, on instruments he names "glorimeters"; who uses as a typical example of production not, as everyone else does, a needle factory, but rather the book industry, paying attention not only to the dissemination of the books themselves, but also to the dissemination of the ideas contained in their pages; who approaches the question of biopower as if economy and ecology were already intertwined; who moves seamlessly from Darwin to Marx and from Adam Smith to Antoine-Augustin Cournot, but without believing for a moment in the usual divisions of economic science; who is interested in luxury, fashions, consumption, quality, labels and recreation as much as he is interested in the military industry and in colonization; who continually uses examples found in the art market, in the dissemination of philosophical ideas, in ethics, and in the law, as if they all counted equally in the production of wealth; who makes science, innovation, innovators, and even idleness itself the basis of economic activity; who spends considerable time following railway tracks, telegraph wires, press publicity, the growth of tourism; who, above all, does not believe in the existence of Capitalism, does not see in the 19th century the terrifying rise of cold calculations and of the reign of the commodity, but on the contrary who defines the growth of markets as that of *passions*; who congratulates the socialists on having created a new *fever* for association and organization.

It is *this* old reactionary we would like to render once again relevant? It is this little bit of economic archeology that we would like to dust off and polish?

Precisely. Let us be honest enough to acknowledge that reading *Das Kapital* would seem quite troubling to us if we had not benefited from over a century of commentaries on it. Everything will initially seem foreign in the economics of Tarde, but perhaps only because it is all new—that, at least, is what we hope to show. Written amidst the first great era of globalization, grappling with all of the technological innovations of the times, taken with the moral and political problem of class struggles, profoundly involved in bio-sociology, founded on quantitative methods which at the time could only be dreamed of but which have today become available thanks to the extension of digitization techniques, it is because it seems freshly minted that we are presenting this work, a century later, in the middle of another period of globalization, at a time of moral, social, financial, political and ecological crisis. This *apax* is not offered as a simple oddity that might interest economic historians, but instead as a document that is essential in order to attain an alternative understanding of our past, and, thus, of our future.

We first considered republishing the two large volumes of *Psychologie Économique*, but were confronted with the extraordinary evolution of the book market—an evolution in itself perfectly Tardian.

Given that the original work is accessible in image format on the Gallica website (http://gallica.bnf.fr/) and in text format (Word or PDF) on the excellent Canadian website *Les classiques des sciences sociales* (http://classiques.uqac.ca/), it would not make much sense to publish it in its entirety, at a prohibitive cost. We have therefore decided to publish this introduction separately, with relatively long quotations, to give readers the desire to turn to the digital versions of the French text to explore it further. In addition, to save those readers who dislike reading on the computer screen and who would rather not overwhelm their printer by printing out the two enormous volumes, we have added on a website a selection of the texts we feel best illustrate the work's importance.

The question Tarde asks himself is quite simple: to what does the surprising notion of political economy that arose in the 18th century correspond? For him, ideas guide the world, and more specifically the ideas economists arrive at concerning the subject of their discipline. To what strange idea of science and of politics does it correspond? For it is indeed a question first of reversing ideas, opinions, and arguments, in order to grasp the change that Tarde proposes to the theory of political economy: yes, for him, the superstructure determines "in the first and in the last instance" the infrastructures, which, in fact, as we shall later see, do not exist.

A strange revolutionary, one might say, this atheistic materialist who, a hundred years before the development of market anthropology, detects in the atheist materialism of the economists of his time, both left and right leaning, a particularly perverse form of a hidden God. Tarde in effect criticizes all those for whom *only a miraculous Providence* seems able to produce automatically, with its invisible or visible hand, the pre-established harmony—whether that of the Market or that of the State, this matters little, because for him, the inventors of political economy agree on nearly everything, and first and foremost on the *existence* of economics as a field in itself. Whereas this is precisely what he disputes.

This lone revolutionary, not linked to any organization or party, with no successors and practically no predecessors, wonders what would happen if we were truly unbelieving, truly *agnostic* when it comes to the subject of economics. "And what if there were in fact no divinity at all ruling over economies?" is really the question he asks. If we agreed once and for all to apply this idea of immanence without any transcendence, could we not once again engage in politics? The politics that the sectarians of Mammon, God of Providence and of automatic Harmony, and that those of the State have been forbidding us from practicing for so long—yes, a politics of *liberty*. Liberalism then? Why should we be afraid to use this word, as long as we remember that its opposite can only be the term "Providentialism"? And what if the choice had never been between Market and State organizations, between liberals and socialists, but instead between those who believe in the miracles of a pre-established harmony and those who refuse to "believe in miracles"? Could we not re-read, retrospectively, everything that has happened to us in the past two hundred years and that we have far too hastily summarized under the name of "capitalism"?

PART I

It Is Because The Economy Is Subjective That It Is Quantifiable

In order to understand Tarde's economic anthropology, we must first accept a complete reversal of our habits: nothing in the economy is objective, all is subjective— or, rather, inter-subjective, and that is *precisely why it can be rendered quantifiable and scientific*. But on condition that we modify what we expect from a science and what we mean by quantifying. These conditions will indeed modify our habits of thought in no small way.

A Return to Value(s)

In an altogether classical way, Tarde begins by defining value. But almost immediately he forces us to change direction. Because value is a highly psychological dimension and one that depends on belief and on desire, it is quantifiable because it possesses a certain intensity:

> It [Value] is a quality, such as color, that we attribute to things, but that, like color, exists only within us by way of a perfectly subjective truth. It consists in the harmonization of the collective judgments we make concerning the aptitude of objects to be more or less—and by a greater or lesser number of people—believed, desired or enjoyed. Thus, this quality belongs among those peculiar ones which, appearing suited to show numerous degrees and to go up or down this ladder without changing their essential nature, merit the name "quantity."

This point is fundamental, and Tarde maintains it beginning in the very first article he published when he was a judge in the small town of Sarlat in the South West of France where he lived most of his life before moving to Paris. To turn the social sciences into true sciences, it is necessary to reach a property that is quantifiable, which, paradoxically, is contained *inside* subjectivities. But although this argument might call to mind the position of marginalists whose point of departure is solidly anchored in individuals, one must never underestimate Tarde's originality. Indeed, never does he put the adjectives "social" and "psychological" in opposition to each other. Despite Durkheim's well-known criticisms of him, what Tarde designates as a psychological phenomenon never refers to anything personal or interior to the subject—what he later calls "intra-psychological" and about which he often asserts that nothing can be said—but always to that which is the most social in us, and which he calls, for this reason, "inter-psychological." As a result, nothing is more foreign to his anthropology than the idea of economic agents cut off from the social world and whose calculations would present clearly-defined boundaries. The words "intimacy" and "subjectivity" must not mislead us: at our most intimate level, it is always the "many" that rules. What makes Tarde so difficult for us to understand, after more than a century of sociologism, is that he never places society and the individual in opposition, but, rather, he sees the two as nothing but temporary aggregates, partial stabilizations, nodes in networks that are completely free of the concepts contained in ordinary sociology.

What is at the basis of the social sciences, in his view, is a kind of *contamination* that moves constantly, from point to point, from individual to individual, but without ever coming to a halt at any specific stop. Subjectivity always refers to the contagious nature of desires and beliefs, which jump from one individual to the next without ever—and here is the crucial point—going through a social context or a structure. The words "social," "psychological," "subjective" and "inter-subjective" are, thus, essentially equivalent, and they all refer to a type of path, a trajectory that demands, for us to be able to follow them, that we never presume the prior existence of a society or of an economic infrastructure, of a general plan distinct from the coming together of its members.

The great advantage of these ways of proceeding is that they immediately bring into plain sight the practical means through which the contagion, the contamination from one point to another, takes place— what Tarde calls "rayons imitatifs" ("imitative rays") in the book that made him famous, *Les Lois de l'imitation* (*The Laws of Imitation*).

This initial definition of the "quantum," which is specific to values, will allow Tarde to unfurl, in lieu of the economy, a fabric made of intertwined relationships, where we must above all be careful not to rush to identify those which are *literally* economic and those that might only be *metaphorically* so. Tarde indeed will continuously show that, on the contrary, economics as a discipline risks losing all scientific objectivity because of a mistaken understanding both of its limits, which are too restrictive, and of its ambitions, which are too vast.

Two Mistakes to Be Avoided

Let us proceed slowly in order to fully grasp the originality of Tarde's position. The notion of value extends first of all to *all assessments of belief and desire*:

> This abstract quantity is divided into three main categories which are the original and essential notions of shared living: truth as a value, utility as a value, and beauty as a value.
>
> The quantitative nature of all of the terms I just listed is just as real as it is scarcely apparent; it is involved in all human judgments. No man, no people has ever failed to seek, as a prize for relentless efforts, a certain growth either of wealth, or glory, or truth, or power, or artistic perfection; nor has he failed to fight against the danger of a *decrease* of all of these assets. We all speak and write as though there existed a scale of these different orders of magnitude, on which we can place different peoples

and different individuals higher or lower and make them rise or fall continuously. Everyone is thus implicitly and intimately convinced that all these things, and not only the first, are, in fact, real quantities. Not to recognize this truly quantitative—if not measurable de jure and de facto— aspect of power, of glory, of truth, of beauty, is thus to go against the constant of mankind and to set as the goal of universal effort a chimera.

There is then a quantitative core which is essential to all of our assessments, no matter the object, and social science must take all of these assessments into account. But, unfortunately, Tarde is quick to add, political economy confused two completely different kinds of quantification: that which is "real and scarcely apparent," and that which is "convenient and apparent" but which reflects only the *extension* of a very small number of calculating instruments intertwined with our passions.

And yet, of all these quantities, only one, wealth, was grasped clearly as such and was considered worthy of being made the subject of a special science: Political Economy. But, even though this object, indeed, given its monetary sign, lends itself to a more mathematical— sometimes even illusory—precision in its speculation, the other terms also each deserve to be studied through a separate science.

The question of the "monetary sign" must be considered extremely carefully. Indeed, Tarde here avoids two symmetrical errors that we too often commit: first, viewing economics as a sort of reduction, one that freezes subjectivity into objectivity; or, conversely, extending this first "reduction" to all activities, even the "highest," believing that one is thus displaying a sharp critical spirit.

Yet, not even once in this book does Tarde complain that economists, "ignoring the wealth of human subjectivity," strive to "quantify all" at the risk of thus "amputating" what is human from its "moral, emotional, aesthetic and social dimensions." His criticism is just the opposite: economists *do not sufficiently quantify* all of the valuations to which they have access. Or, rather, they do not go back far enough, along a continuum, towards the intersection of the tensors and vectors of desire and belief that lie at the heart, we might say, of social *matter*.

> But the economist neglects to recognize that there is no wealth either, whether agricultural, industrial or other, that cannot be considered from the point of view of either the knowledge it involves, the powers it grants, the rights of which it is a product, or its more or less aesthetic or unaesthetic character.

But the opposite mistake would be to think that Tarde extends the quantifications of wealth ordinarily accepted in economics to the *metaphorical* analysis of truths, glories, powers, ethics, rights and arts, in the manner of Pierre Bourdieu, by the increased use of the terms capital, interest, calculation and profit, whether qualifying them as "symbolic" or not. Once again, it is the reverse: the quantifiable root that will allow for the founding of a true economic science lies first of all in the complex interplay between trust and mistrust, and *only then*, out of convenience and simplification, transported into the relatively simplified case of the "exchange of assets." One could almost say that, in the generalized economics that he puts forward, it is the political economy of wealth that represents its metaphorical extension, or rather its metonymic narrowing—a tiny part being taken for the whole. Tarde proposes, instead, to extend economics to *all* valuations, without, however, being limited to following the very small number of valuations that people have learned, for the sake of convenience, to measure in terms of money.

Ceasing to Confuse Recto with Verso

It is only once we understand the extent to which he avoids making these two mistakes (the lament against quantification, on the one hand, and the metaphorical extension of calculations of wealth to other forms of "symbolic" value, on the other) that we can measure the audacity, originality and fertility of the following statement:

> It is my intention to show, to the contrary, that, if we wish to come to true and, consequently, genuinely scientific laws in political economy, we must turn over, so to speak, the always useful but slightly worn garment of the old schools, turn it inside out, bring to light that which was hidden and ask the signified for an explanation of the signifier, and ask the human spirit for an explanation of social materials.

How can we explain the fact that economists made such a serious mistake concerning the recto and verso of their science? The reason given by Tarde goes along with what market anthropologists have shown again and again over the past decade or so: no relationship is economic without there being an extension of the calculation techniques of economists—in the broadest sense of the word. The field of *economics*, invented in the 18th century, did not discover a continent; instead, it built one from scratch, or, rather, organized one, conquered it, and it colonized it. To quote Michel Callon's powerful phrase, it is the economic discipline that frames and shapes the economy as an entity: *"without economics, no economy."* Contrary to the robinsonades of the 18th century, and just as Karl Polanyi and later Marshal Sahlins had so skillfully shown, man is not born an economist, he becomes one. On condition, however, that he is surrounded by enough instruments and enough calculative devices to render otherwise imperceptible differences visible and readable. To practice economics is not to reveal the anthropological essence of humanity; it is to organize in a certain way something elusive. Neither is it, as we shall soon see, to uncover the true nature of humanity.

In order to understand how the work of economists *formats* relationships which, without them, would have entirely different forms, we must accurately grasp the small *supplement* contributed by the invention of calculation devices and, in particular, standards such as currency.

Wealth is something much simpler and more easily measured; for it comprises infinite degrees and very few different types, with ever decreasing differences. So that the gradual replacement of the nobility by wealth, of aristocracy by plutocracy, tends to render the social status increasingly subject to numbers and measures.

If all of Proust's subtlety is required to place the differences in social rank between Swann and Madame Verdurin on a value scale, this attention to detail is no longer necessary in order to classify the world's billionaires—any run-of-the-mill *Fortune* journalist would have no trouble doing so—once measurements take the form of credit and capital. We must be careful, though: this does not mean that we have become plutocratic, that the dominance of commodity has been broadened, that numbers in monetary quantity are encroaching on the real and material infrastructure that seems to underlie the economy as an entity. Not at all: the measure having become "simpler," "social status" has, as a result, become easier to identify. So it is indeed appropriate to distinguish between two types of measurement, one that captures the real state, which we could call *measured* measurement, to distinguish it from the type that formats the social world and that we could call *measuring* measurement. This distinction allows us to see that there are indeed other instruments available to make the economy truly quantifiable.

> Now, a man's glory, no less than his credit, no less than his fortune, is to increase or decrease without changing in its nature. It is, therefore, a sort of social quantity.... Priests and the religious have studied the factors involved in the production (meaning here reproduction) of beliefs, of "truths", with no less care than that with which economists study the reproduction of wealth. They could give us lessons on the practices best suited to sowing the faith (retreats, forced meditation, preaching), and on the readings, the conversations, and the types of conduct that weaken it.

Let us introduce the term *valuemeter* to describe all of the devices which make visible and readable the value judgments that form the foundation of what Tarde calls economics. It is easy to imagine how interested he would be in the current era, in which we see growing numbers of new ways of "obtaining data," in the form of audience ratings, polls, marketing surveys, shows like *American Idol*, competitions, rankings, auctions, spying, clicks of the mouse, etc.—new means of gathering data which are very precious for "rendering the social status increasingly subject to numbers and measures." One might almost say that it was Tarde's bad luck to have lived a full century before the "quali-quantitative" types of data that are today made more and more numerous through new information and communication systems. It is said of Tarde that he indulges in a mere "literary" sociology, and that is indeed true: he wanted desires and beliefs to be quantified, while the statistics of his day—which he knew well, having headed the Institute of Statistics of the Justice Ministry—were far too rudimentary to capture them. Today's wave of digitization should make us perhaps much more attentive to Tarde's argument.

How to Specify Quantities

Let us, however, take care to correctly understand his thought: everything is potentially a number, because valuemeters only gather, concentrate, extract and simplify subtle weighings, innumerable "logical duels" that constantly occur within us when we encounter those to whom we have strong attachments and whom we need in order to exist. In other words, Tarde does not claim that the calculation devices used by economists perform the social, in a way comparable to what a waffle-maker would do to batter, shapeless in itself, poured in by the ladle. For him, there already exists in the batter, dare we say, a particular type of quantum that has only an *indirect* link to what economists call the quantifiable. It is precisely this indirect aspect that explains why they were so often mistaken when trying to render their discipline more scientific and why they confused heads and tails. Once again, it is not a question of complaining about economists and their mania for quantifying, which would have applied the same standard of comprehension to all subjects. On the contrary, argues Tarde, one must lament the fact that they do not have enough of a taste for quantification to seek out, in each type of practice, the tensors that are specific to it. Tarde argues that the very places economists may have failed in their quantification reveal a number of interesting things regarding the other types of quantification which are just waiting to be brought to light, provided we make the effort to go and seek them out.

All of the other instruments available to make economics truly quantifiable constitute the best proof that there is a vast reserve of quantification.

> There are indeed other measures: each type of statistic is one. The rise or fall in popularity of a public figure is measured fairly accurately through voting statistics.

What counts—literally—is the comparison of judgments. This process is in no way connected to money as such; it is found in all valuemeters and all glorimeters. That is why it is easy to follow the growing comparison in two domains that an economist would likely separate but that Tarde has no trouble linking, such as the press and currency:

> [...] The development of the press had the effect of giving moral values a quantitative character that was more and more marked and better and better suited to justify their comparison with the exchange value. The latter, which must also have been quite confused in the centuries before the common use of currency, became better defined as currency spread and became more unified. It was then able to give rise, for the first time, to political economy. Similarly, before the advent of the daily press, the notions of the scientific or literary value of writing, of people's fame and reputation, were still vague, as the awareness of their gradual waxings and wanings could barely be felt; but with the development of the press, these ideas became clearer, were accentuated, became worthy of being the objects of philosophical speculations of a new sort.

The originality of drawing such a parallel is clear: Tarde does not say that the press is subject to the "deleterious influence of the powers of money"; the connection between the two domains does not pass through the required step of searching for hidden forces in infrastructures—as we shall see, there is not, for Tarde, any infrastructure at all. The connection between the two domains is infinitely more intimate. Tarde compares two styles of trajectory and contamination, both of which—the first one several centuries ago and the second right before our eyes—allow us to identify the instrumentation through which we move from a local, individual and impractical system of quantification to one that is generalized, rapid, and reflexive. Credit and credibility require accounting instruments or, to use a term that is not Tarde's but that defines precisely the movement of inter-comparison, they need *metrology*. Valuemeters connected together, little by little, end up building metrological chains which make the inter-comparison of subjectivities increasingly "precise," "accentuated," and "worthy of being objects of speculations of a new sort." And, among these speculations, Tarde never fails to include the sociology of science, a typical case of a metrology of learned literature, made visible and readable by the very extension of the quasi-currency we call credibility where, better than anywhere else, the very production of the finely differentiated degrees of belief plays out.

> How is a man's credit, his fame and his glory, born, and how does it grow in all of its forms? It is indeed worth looking at these different forms of production, as well as the production of wealth and of its venal value.... If there are any "natural laws" that regulate the manufacture of these or those items in greater or lesser quantities and the increase or decrease of their venal value, why would there not be one that would regulate the appearance, growth, increase or decrease of the popular enthusiasm for this or that man, of the royalist loyalty of a people, of its religious faith, of its trust in this or that institution?

If you really want to quantify—which is, after all, the foundation of all sciences—you should try to find all the available types of quantum, instead of using just one to analyze all the others. The quantification of glory is as good a measure of wealth as wealth is of faith, or as faith is of enthusiasm, and so forth. Users of Google will have no difficulty understanding what digitization has done to the calculation of authority, the mapping of credibility and the quantification of glory.

Quantifying, Yes, but Doing So Advisedly

We now understand the confusion of economists as Tarde sees them: while they may have been right to seek to quantify, they misidentified the source that could have allowed them to give certainty to their discipline at last. Their mistake consisted in the following: they took for a "measured measure" the "measuring measure" allowed by an extension of the chains of inter-comparison. This extension itself was due to an entirely different phenomenon than the one they believed they were observing. They in fact thought that progress in economics had to be progress in detachment, distance and objectivity.

> To be as objective and abstract as one could: that was the method... The ideal was to conceal under abstractions such as credit, service and work, the sensations and feelings underlying them, so that no one could notice them, and to treat these abstractions as objects: real and material objects analogous to the objects treated by the chemist or the physicist and, as with them, falling under the law of number and measurement. Thus, the rubric of money and finances, where this twofold ideal seems to be realized, where everything seems to be denumerable and measurable just as in physics and chemistry, has always been the economists' hobbyhorse.

As a measuring measure, money is, of course, excellent, but what it measures, or rather what it registers in a simplified manner to make it easier to capture, has no kind of link with what is indicated in the numbers. Not, as the perpetual humanist critics of economics believe, because "the human heart cannot be reduced to calculation," but, on the contrary, because the human heart calculates and compares constantly, but on a *different* scale and through very different, less readable and less contrasting weights. This is why Tarde continues the previous sentence and proposes that we shift our attention towards the true source of all other measures:

> It remains true that value, of which money is but the sign, is nothing, absolutely nothing, if not a combination of entirely subjective things, of beliefs and desires, of ideas and volitions, and that the peaks and troughs of values in the stock market, unlike the oscillations of a barometer, could not even remotely be explained without considering their psychological causes: fits of hope or discouragement in the public, propagation of a good or bad sensational story in the minds of speculators.

So, here we find the explanation of the recto/verso inversion which might have seemed, when we introduced it earlier, a gratuitous defiance on the part of Tarde.

> It is not that economists have entirely ignored this subjective aspect of their subject... this subjective aspect has always been regarded as the verso and not the recto of economic science. The masters of this discipline have wrongly believed, I repeat, that a dominant, or even exclusive, preoccupation with the external side of things

could alone raise their observations to the dignity of a scientific corpus. Even when they had to directly envisage the psychological side of the phenomena they investigated—the motivations of the worker or the needs of the consumer, for example—they conceived of a human heart so simplified and so schematic: so to speak, a human soul so mutilated that this minimum of indispensable psychology had the air of a mere postulate fated to support the geometric unfolding of their deductions.

If we had quoted this passage at the beginning of our essay, it would have seemed like the usual lament against economists' mania for quantifying, whereas we must understand it, instead, as a call to look *everywhere*, and especially *elsewhere*, for the valuemeters capable of capturing "human souls" when they evaluate their good and their evil, when they believe, when they desire, when they pray, when they want, when they become intertwined. It is on this new and shifted basis that Tarde offers the different social sciences a kind of *new deal*:

[...] Political economy, thus surrounded, would lose, it is true, its mysterious isolation as an unstable block cast in the desert of an as-yet-unborn sociology, by metaphysicians or logicians. It would, however, gain by appearing in its true place as a social science, and by seeing its everyday notions, its divisions, and its theories, controlled by the sister-sciences which would be illuminated by its light and would illuminate it with theirs.

Needless to say, intellectual history did not take this pact in any way seriously, and people continued for a century to hold onto the relatively absurd idea that *economics* as a discipline had miraculously discovered underneath it a submerged frozen continent, the *economy*, governed by rigid laws and which had the unheard-of ability to freeze the superstructures built on top of it. Among the social sciences, economics alone was to be considered truly scientific because it alone had succeeded in reaching the rational and objective core of the human soul.

A Mistake in Temperature

How can we summarize Tarde's innovation so as to remember that the question is indeed one of quantifying the economy, albeit by shifting it entirely into the realm of inter-subjectivity—the only means, paradoxically, by which it can be rendered somewhat scientific? First of all, by avoiding another epistemological error, which is also, as we shall see later, a serious political error: the mistake of thinking that the more valuemeters and metrological chains there are, the more economic history moves from passion to reason, from the irrational to the rational, from the warmth of traditional haggling to the "economic horror" of "neo-liberal" markets.

> Will we say that the progress of reason, the supposed companion of the progress of civilization, takes responsibility for realizing little by little the abstraction imagined by economists, stripping concrete man of all the motives for action besides the motive of personal interest? But nothing lets us suppose this and there is not a single aspect of social life in which one does not see passion grow and unfold together with intelligence... So it is in the economic world, and nowhere, not even here, do I perceive traces

of a refrigerating transformation of man in a less and less passionate and more and more rational direction.

The new economies observed by Tarde from his Chair at the Collège de France, that of class struggles, of the first great globalization movement, of the massive migrations of men, of frenzied innovations punctuated by the great World Fairs, and the carving up of the colonial empires, in no way demonstrated the advent of reason. Rather, it presented a spectacle of:

> [...] passions of unprecedented intensity, prodigious ambitions of conquest, a sort of new religion, socialism, and a proselytising fervour unknown since the primitive Church. These are the interests, the passionate interests, which it is a question of making agree with one another and with the equally passionate interests of billionaire capitalists, no less inebriated with the hope of winning, the pride of life, and the thirst for power.

What, then, is economics? We can now define it as the "science of passionate interests."

We must not misunderstand this, though. Tarde is not saying that, alas, calculating economic reason finds itself distorted, kidnapped and perturbed by passions, coalitions, contaminations and rumors which prevent its calculations from being correct; he is not saying that, if, by some impossible miracle, we were able to rid ourselves of all of this irrational jumble, we would finally recover economic reason. No, *everything* in economics is irrational, *everything* in economics is, we might say, extra-economic (in the everyday sense of the word). And this is because it is made up of passions whose astonishing development in the 19th century only amplified their interconnections. It is precisely this intertwining that economists simultaneously caught sight of and, amazingly, fled immediately with horror, as though they had seen the head of Gorgon.

In inventing homo economicus, economists have engaged in a double abstraction. First, the unwarranted one of having conceived of a man with nothing human in his heart; second, of having represented this individual as detached from any group, corporation, sect, party, homeland, or association of any sort. This second simplification is no less mutilating than the first, whence it derives. Never, in any period of history, have a producer and a consumer, a seller and a buyer been in each other's presence without having first been united to one another by some entirely sentimental relation—being neighbours, sharing citizenship or religious communion, enjoying a community of civilization—and, second, without having been, respectively, escorted by an invisible cortege of associates, friends, and coreligionists whose thought has weighed on them in the discussion of prices or wages, and has finally won out, most often to the detriment of their strictly individual interest. Never, indeed, not even in the first half of the nineteenth century—which is nevertheless the sole period in the history of labor conditions in which every workers' corporation in France seemed to have been destroyed—did the worker appear free from every formal or moral commitment to his comrades, in the presence of a boss himself entirely disengaged from strict obligations or propriety towards his own colleagues or even his own rivals.

The attachments are what must be quantified; how could this have been forgotten? It will be argued that institutional economics, the economics of conventions, has for years accepted such imbroglios as fact. That may be true, but Tarde's book was published in 1902! Why did we lose a century? This is all the more striking because Tarde goes much further than today's cautious researchers who are content to correct the Ptolemaic system of the pure and perfect market by adding to it a multitude of epicycles turning in all directions—contracts, trust, information, rules, norms, and coalitions. Yet, much like Copernicus had no one to read his book, Tarde already placed the quantitative focus elsewhere. There is no Providence in this "invisible cortege of associates," and certainly not that of harmonizing reason. Tarde's ambition, all the more radical seeing as it does not lean on any school, consists indeed in making the cycles of passionate interests revolve around a different sun, a sun which sheds light and burns—which sheds light *because* it burns.

Getting Closer Instead of Moving Away

To fully grasp this point, we must agree to give up one last epistemological pretension, that of *distance* and *exteriority*. Having reached this point, Tarde, ever courteous, allows himself a touch of irony regarding the acrobatic maneuvers economists perform in order to get as far away as possible from precisely the phenomena that they have the chance of being in close contact with, and which, as a result, should jump out at them! The argument, which is completely counter-intuitive, merits further analysis. Tarde begins by distinguishing between two types of psychology, not in relation to the nature of the objects to which they are applied, but in relation to the degree of *proximity* we have to them.

> The eminently psychological nature of the social sciences, of which political economy is but a branch, would have given rise to fewer objections had the distinction been made between two psychologies that are normally blended into one.... it is useful to note that the objects of the self can be either natural things, *unfathomable in their hermetically sealed inner depths*, or other selves, other spirits where the self is reflected by its external manifestation and learns to know itself better by discovering others. The latter objects of the self, which are simultaneously subjects like it, give rise to an entirely exceptional relationship between them and it, which carves sharply, in high relief, among the usual relationships of the self with the entities of nature, minerals, plants, and even lower species of animals.... they are the only objects captured from the inside, because their intimate nature is the very one of which the subject observing them is conscious. However, when the self looks at minerals or stars, material substances of any sort, whether organic or inorganic, the forces that produced these forms can only be guessed at by hypothesis, and only their outward sign is perceived.

This surprising difference between the human world and the natural world, one that does not divide according to the usual distinction between the symbolic world, on the one hand, and the material world, on the other, can be found in all of Tarde's work. Let us remember that, for Tarde, "everything is society": stars, cells, bodies, political groups, the lively firings of the brain. "Material," for Tarde, therefore first and foremost means "social." Could he have been a socio-biologist (or as they said at the time, bio-soci-ologist)? Could he have committed the sin of natural-ization? Or worse, that of social Darwinism? No, because there is a difference in capture and not in nature between the objects called material and the subjects of society: we can see the former from *afar*, *roughly*, and *from the outside*; whereas we see the latter from *up close*, *in small numbers*, and *from the inside*!

> Thus, we understand very well that, when it is a question of studying the relationships of the self with natural beings and of establishing the physical sciences, including even biology, the self tries its best to systematically forget itself as much as possible, to put the least of itself and of the personal impressions it receives from the outside, in the notions it conceives of matter, of force and of life, to resolve, if possible, all of nature in terms of extension and points in motions, in geometrical notions, whose origin, also utterly psychological, only reveals itself to very prac-ticed analytical eyes and in fact does not involve their psychological nature at all.

Tarde does not claim that economists would be wrong to treat human objects like natural objects under the pretext that, as is so often said, that which is human "eludes nature and objectivity." He willingly acknowl-edges that there are excellent reasons, in physics, in chemistry, or in biology, to take the associations of enti-ties from the outside as statistical clouds, subject to external forces which govern them. But if we adopt this perspective in many cases, it is because we cannot grasp them from close enough, as we are not able to penetrate into their innermost beings. Even if their "origin," like that of all monads, is psychological and made up of relationships, their "nature," seen from a distance and as a whole, no longer appears to be such. In any case, there would be no advantage, no epistemological gain, in making such a supposition. And here he is, drawing the following stunning conclusion:

> But is this a reason, when the moment comes to study the reciprocal relationships of selves—that is, to establish the social sciences—for the self to continue to try to run away from itself, and to take as a model for its new sciences the sciences of nature? By the most exceptional of privileges, he finds himself, in the social world, seeing clearly to the bottom of those beings whose relationships he studies, holding in his hands the hidden drives of the actors, and yet he would gladly give up this advantage to be able to model himself after the physicist or the naturalist who, not having it, is forced to do without it and to compensate for it as he can!"

"To run away from itself"? We understand the horror that Durkheim felt when he learned of the work of his elder. If there is, for Tarde, a mistake to be avoided, it is to take social facts "as things," whereas, in the other sciences, if we take things "as things," it is for lack of a better alternative! How could sociologists and, even more surprisingly, economists, have had the crazy idea of wanting to imitate physicists and biologists through an entirely artificial effort at distancing, while the very thinkers they tried to imitate would give their right hands to find themselves at last close to particles, cells, frogs, bodies with whom they try to come into intimate association with the help of their instruments? Why do economists run away by giving themselves a certain distance which any researcher would wish to eliminate, at the risk of losing the long dreamt of opportunity to understand the social, while the others, the "true" scholars, try at all costs, with the invention of all sorts of instruments, to *come nearer* to that which is at a distance from them?

Here indeed is the core, the difficult, technical and ever new point of Tarde's proposition: if we can distinguish, in any given aggregate, associates, on the one hand, and laws, structures, and rules, on the other, it is because we are forced to ignore what shapes them from the inside through the swarming of assessments and battles of logic. To put it bluntly, the notion of structure is a makeshift one, an artifact of our ignorance, itself due to our having too great a distance with what we study. We shall show, further on, the surprising political consequences Tarde will deduce from this point, which remains, a hundred years later, an incomprehensible paradox for the majority of the social sciences. For the moment, let us understand that he will, unlike economists, make as much as possible of "this exceptional privilege" that makes it possible to capture the "hidden drives" that connect us to goods, without having to hypothesize about "natural laws" which would, *in addition*, give shape to these attachments. It is thanks to this privilege that Tarde invents a sociology and an economics which will be able to do without any transcendence. He will not flee in the face of economics. He wants us to look at the head of Gorgon head-on.

But, one might wonder, economists are no fools, so why did they try to imitate an epistemology which distanced them so from their project of quantification in thinking that they were imitating the exact sciences whose *libido sciendi* they were in fact reversing?

Tarde's answer to this is very similar to that of Karl Polanyi, and he draws, in fact, from the same source through a Sismondi quote. There have to be very powerful political reasons in order to suspend all common sense and to reverse all principles of method in this way.

> Why did economists conceive of the object of their science in its most material aspects? Sismondi answers: "It was, he says, from the science of finance that was born that of political economy, through an order that was the reverse of the natural progression of ideas. Philosophers wanted to protect the population from the plundering ravages of absolute power; they felt that, to make themselves heard, they needed to speak to the rulers of their *interests* and not of justice and duty; they tried to show them clearly what the nature and the causes of the wealth of nations were, to teach them to share it without destroying it." That is one reason why political economy, from its beginnings, took on such a positive color, and decided, due to their own bias, to disregard any psychological or moral consideration.

An entire discipline, thousands of departments, hundreds of thousands of MBA's, to protect us from the ravages of "absolute power"? All of that, to protect one's property? The invention of an entire impersonal science to avoid favoring people? A disinterested science of interest, entirely based on the defense of interests? We understand the reason, but, for heaven's sake, pleads Tarde, let us not confuse this convenient solution with the demands of a science that deserved better. Now we must invert the inversion, put economics upright again and let it walk at last on its own two feet: the ideas that guide the world (and in particular those of economists, who perform passions and interests) and the valuemeters which reflect their movement and accentuate their readability. We must stop confusing economics, the *discipline*—the word has never been more fitting—and the economy. The choice has to be made between *economics* and *economy*. The latter still remains an unknown continent because the former, busy performing it, has continuously fled its true composition.

PART II
The Nature of Economics

By inverting the economists' inversion of a science invented for reasons too strictly political, Tarde opens up a continent which still remains, a century later, largely unknown, the continent of the *attachments to goods and bads*, which he wants to place at the heart of the discipline he intends to re-found and which he names "economic psychology." But where should this continent be situated? Surely not *above* the law, ethics, aesthetics, and mores, like an infrastructure whose cold objectivity would obey calculable laws. Of course, there are indeed laws, there are indeed calculations, there are indeed objectifications, but all of this circulates like the rest—we now understand—by contagion, following along the networks of inter-comparison, *as far away* as there are economists, both professional and amateur, *as long as* accounting techniques are being invented, developed and maintained. All of this infrastructure is *added* to the associations of people and goods whose judgments it simplifies in part, but which, in part, it complicates further.

Yet, if one no longer believes that economics has captured the deep meaning of the economy which it had been content simply to format, how should one approach the task of elaborating a social science capable of seizing both the formatting of the economic sciences and that which constantly *escapes* this same formatting?

Invention Before Accumulation

The solution Tarde offers to this question may seem fairly perplexing to us: it consists in thrusting the economy back into the general movement of monads he developed in his other works. The pullulating of living societies whose intertwining forms the texture of the world is not chaotic but ends up by creating interferences, rhythms, and amplifications, on condition that one agrees to discern three stages in this proliferation: the *repetition* of a first difference, the *opposition* created by the repetition, and, finally, the *adaptation* making it possible for it to temporarily get out of these oppositions thanks to new differentiations. We must be careful not to read into this movement a return of Hegel's dialectic. No superior law guides this world towards a denouement through the play of negativity and contradiction. There is, contrary to the notebooks of the young Marx, no adventure of subject and object at play in these issues of capital and labor. Let us not forget what Tarde says against all philosophy of identity as contradiction: "To exist is to differ."

As a result, the supreme law for him is not negation—and even less the negation of negation—but rather *invention*, which, once repeated obstinately, brings about countless struggles, which can only be gotten out of through other inventions. Fifty years before Joseph Schumpeter, eighty years before the development of the economics of technical change, Tarde places innovation and the monitoring of inventions at the heart of his doctrine. Follow innovations from the mesh woven in the brain of individuals—a brain itself conceived, as we have seen, as a mass of neurons; analyze by which canals they spread; document the conflicts they give rise to when they enter into a struggle with those innovations previously repeated; observe how they end up combining, piling up one on top of the other, adjusting themselves, and you will have the whole economy, whether it be of new religious convictions, new plants, new legal codes, railways, financial tools, or political opinions.

> The problem can be summed up as follows: to grasp as closely as possible the genesis of inventions and the laws of imitations. Economic progress supposes two things: on the one hand, a growing number of different desires, for, without a difference in desires, no exchange is possible, and, with the appearance of each new, different desire, the life of exchange is kindled. On the other hand, a growing number of similar exemplars of each desire taken separately, for, without this similitude, no industry is possible, and, the more this similitude expands or prolongs itself, the more production is widened or reinforced.

The notion of accumulation does not do justice to this process of differentiation. It describes a phase—but only a phase—of the industry during which only the author of the repetition is active. It only marks a moment, albeit one necessary to development, which allows markets to grow, but never to change paths. It is also the product of an economic science—starting with economic sociology—which treats entities—humans and assets, services and technologies—as interchangeable, since they are seen from a distance, without capturing the small differences that would explain that change is not an exogenous shock suddenly befalling monomaniacal capitalists. This is what Tarde criticizes in Darwin:

> His mistake [...] seems to me to have been in relying far more on the struggle for existence, a biological form of opposition, than on cross-breading and hybridization, biological forms of adaptation and harmony. A function just as important as the production of a new species would not be able to be a continuous and daily function, while the simple production of a new individual—generation—is an intermittent function. An *exceptional phenomenon*, and not a daily phenomenon, must be at the base of this specific novelty. And [...] a fertile hybridization, as an exception, is far neater than a hereditary accumulation of small advantageous variations, through competition and selection, to explain the formation of new types of life.

If accumulation is not the relevant point of entry to understand the dynamics of the economy, one must look elsewhere. The interference and intersection of the paths of desire which inhabit individuals are much better suited to provide information on the probability of inflexion points. Herein lies the problem of the notion of accumulation: it does not provide information on the *intensities* of the economy.

> When, at the crucial moment, on a battlefield, just the right glance from the general lets an uncertain victory tilt to one side, the victory is due to this sudden idea, not to the accumulation of the prior efforts. And when, out of a thousand researchers, a single one, through a sudden intuition, discovers the solution to the enigma posed to all, it is not the long and sterile efforts of the others, not even the duration and intensity of his own efforts—often lesser than theirs—to which credit for the discovery should be given.

Accumulation is not a good candidate, and effort alone guarantees nothing. So what are economists left with to explain the shapes of the economy? Genius, of course, but a type of genius that is attained first of all through the interference of all the lines of imitation. Genius does not guarantee anything; it is simply a quick way to sum up what we have observed, not what we may predict. In hindsight, the unique configuration which brings into existence the solution to a recalcitrant mathematical problem, or the general's glance that saves his troops from death, now that is where genius lies; it does not reside at all in the author of the theorem, nor in the general himself. Tarde mentions genius fairly often as if he gave importance to the outer wrapping of the individual "genius," but this is a linguistic simplification and a way of evoking the ability to compose using lines of influence. Genius is not a point of departure; it is no more a place of action than it is one of passion. It is more precisely a moment of incandescence that can only ever be described, never recreated. Here again, Tarde does not set up an opposition between the mysterious origin of the individual genius and the slavish imitation of past models. He shifts levels: a genius is an individual in whom the multitudes of repetitions and imitations (those lively firings of the brain) lead, dare we say, a life of their own.

Let us note, in passing, that trade, which so often serves as a pillar for the economic robinsonnades of the 19th century, does not find its place in Tarde's economics. Trade does indeed exist, but it is brought back to its proper role in the genealogy of markets. What launches a market, what builds an economy, is not trade, which is but a zero-sum game; it is rather the pooling and the coordinating of previously scattered energies. Tarde places faith and trust at the center of this pooling effort.

> Only half of the truth is being told in seeing the trade contract as the essential and seminal economic event. Trade, in truth, favors and develops directly only consumption. The direct agent of production is another contract, which is no less seminal and no less fundamental: the loan contract. Through trade, we do each other favors, but all while defying one another: give and take; through loans, we place trust in one another.

Thus, we can see a very singular relationship between faith and invention: a shared movement consisting in connecting and gathering previously separate entities. It is necessary for there to be trust for the first transactions to come into being; it is necessary to loosen the fixation of *Homo economicus* on the lure of profit because there needs to be also passion and risk-taking in order to bring the economy towards new paths through the emergence of small differences. Trust, much like invention, creates new groupings; it folds the economy in a certain way which will then be confirmed through repetition.

Difference and Repetition is both the title of Gilles Deleuze's thesis and Tarde's fundamental principle. Invention produces differences; repetition allows for their diffusion; conflict is inevitable; no pre-established harmony allows for a solution (as we shall later see): it is necessary to invent yet other solutions in order to temporarily generate other innovations, which, by repeating themselves, will produce other differences, and the cycle will begin again. That is the fundamental rhythm, the back beat that, alone, allows economic activity to acquire realism. What we need to follow in order to establish an economic science are "states of mind" and "logical duels."

> From salesman to client, from client to salesman, from consumer to consumer and from producer to producer, whether competing or not, there is a continuous and invisible transmission of feelings—an exchange of persuasions and excitement through conversations, through newspapers, through example—which precedes commercial exchanges, often making them possible, and which always helps to set their conditions.

The fabric of vectors and tensors which defines the attachments of people and assets consists—and here lies Tarde's truly innovative character—of arguments whose premises and deductions form *practical syllogisms* which are, in fact, the whole substance of economics.

> Either through authoritarian suggestion or through demonstration, we can only communicate our thoughts to others (which is equivalent to a gift of assets, the unilateral beginning of an exchange of goods) on condition that we present them through their measurable and quantitative aspects. If it is a question of forcing our judgment into someone else's head, through demonstration, we will need a more or less explicit syllogism, that is a relationship between species and genus or between genus and species, established between two ideas, which means that one is included in the other, is of the same type (undetermined or determined but real) of things which are similar, and perceived as similar, that the other, the general proposition, encompasses and contains.

For Tarde, the economic matter—this is what remains so difficult for us—is a real force because it is a rhetorical power: it is indeed a question of persuasion, syllogism and conviction. Or, rather, rhetoric attains in it such power because it encroaches, so to speak, on the ability of the monads themselves to assess and to calculate. It is because of this background of "calculable forces" that the addition of calculative devices, of metrological chains, can have such a performative, explicatory capacity, that they can even become forces of production. It is because the monads calculate at all times and in all possible manners that the addition of calculative devices, which are minuscule prostheses, brings about such a prodigious amplification of evaluations. Tarde's cleverness lies in adding, to the intertwining of calculations, the decisive role of theories and doctrine.

Nowhere can his acumen be better seen than on the widely-discussed subject of "fair price." At no time does he think it possible to appeal to nature—to natural law—in order to establish the difference with "real price," but neither does he ever have recourse to the objectivity simply of the markets to define this price.

> Economists, in viewing as the natural or normal price the price to which the freest, most unbridled competition leads, believed they were in so doing eliminating the bothersome idea of *fair price*. But, in reality, all they did was to *justify* in this way the real prices precisely, often the most abusive ones, formed under the tyrannical rule of the strongest. And the problem is that this way of seeing things, which is in itself an unconscious way of conceiving of fair price all while denying it, in fact acts, in quite a regrettable way, on real price. When everyone has been persuaded, on the strength of the work of ancient economists, that the price automatically determined by the "free play of supply and demand" is justice itself, there is no doubt that this general belief plays a part in making it possible for exorbitant prices, or prices so minimal that public conscience would have rejected them other times, to be established without protest, or even with general approval.

As always for Tarde, the sciences do more than just know: they add themselves to the world, they involve it, they fold it, they complicate it on numerous points all while simplifying it on others—but we should never assume that we can trust them to eliminate morality, that "bothersome idea" of social justice. Even if one succeeds, through scientific claim, in aligning power struggles, or objective science and the nature of things, the fact remains that millions of gaps, judgments, small differences, and criticisms would force everyone to reevaluate the relation between the "justified price" and the "fair price."

Besides, how can we deny the action of the idea that each period or each country has on what is just as regards price? To what type of consumption is morality entirely foreign, if by morality we mean the superior and profound rule of conduct in accordance with the major convictions and passions which guide life? And, if we set aside these convictions and these dominating passions which, silent or conscious, are the social and individual forces par excellence, what are we explaining in political economy?

Nothing will cool passionate interests. Imagining an economy that is wise at last, reigning coolly over individuals who are rational and reasonable at last, ruled by good governance, is like imagining an ecological system with no animals, plants, viruses, or earthworms.

A Social Darwinism, But an Inverted One

As should be clear by now, this model takes after Darwin more than after Hegel. One might argue that the whole second half of the 19th century was Darwinian. But Tarde understands immediately, thanks to his metaphysics of difference, that Darwinism, that ultimate remedy against all Providentialism, immediately becomes a poison—social Darwinism—as soon as one surreptitiously adds to it, *in addition* to the monads, an artificial structure, a master plan, a finality, a design. All is invention, multiplicity and repetition, but the latter are guided by no plan, no dialectic, no finality. It is precisely concerning the living, those close to us, that we must above all not start to separate those who organize from those who are organized. Tarde is one of the rare thinkers of the 19th century to have "registered" Darwinism without immediately stifling his discoveries through the addition of an artificial transcendence: evolution as a creator, the optimum, natural selection of the fittest. Here is indeed yet another example of Tarde's originality: in his view, to naturalize always means to un-objectify in order to "inter-subjectify," and, by the same token, to pull economic activity away from scientific claims. That is why he immediately sees how to extract Darwin's poison and to keep only the remedy to the serious sickness which consists in seeing, to use the American expression, *intelligent design* in the living.

We know well that the touchstone, in economics as well as in biology, is always the question of competition, of aggression. It is always possible to tell the true from the false Darwinist by the pleasure he takes in justifying (or not) economic competition through stories of wolves, foxes, bonobos or praying mantises. Whereas, Tarde, with a perfectly steady hand, always keeps us from mistaking competition for something other than a particular moment between invention and adaptation. There is no ambiguity on this point: economists, just like naturalists, must all be reexamined so that we might grasp what "nature" can really offer us.

This mistake, without a doubt, is not limited to economists. They borrowed it from the naturalists who were for a long time seduced, in grand fashion it is true, by the paradoxical idea of seeing in the continuous battle of the living the fundamental cause of life's progress, and in the generalized murder of individuals the very creation of species. And, certainly, it is good that Darwin's genius pushed this paradox to its limit, for, at present, it is still established that natural selection, that excellent agent of purifying elimination, does not create anything and posits that which it claims to explain—living renovations—in the form of individual variations, and that the secret of these creations of life are hidden from our eyes in the depths of the fertilized egg instead of consisting in the outer shock of organisms fighting each other.... Do we not see what the gradual propagation of the struggle for existence and of natural selection unleashed in terms of ferocious coveting between nations and classes? There had to be a society saturated by the law of force, correctly or not deduced from these hypotheses, to make possible this enormous number of assaults against the weak or the defeated which, under the name of colonial politics or class struggles, our European statesmen already practice and our theoreticians justify in advance.

There isn't the shadow of acquiescence, as we can see, with the naturalization of the struggle for life. One would have to wait for half a century and for the brilliant work of Polanyi to find the same degree of indignation against the alarming sophism of a deceptive economics justified by an equally deceptive view of biology. But Tarde goes further than Polanyi, for he wants to remedy the errors of biology as well, and to purge not only economics but *nature* itself of all Providentialism:

[The mistake] is not only apt to skew the spirit, but also to corrupt the heart. It consists in believing, essentially, that, behind the cloth where human events are woven, there is a sort of Mephistophelian, unsettling irony, that enjoys making good come from evil and evil come from good, in endowing murderous hatred, exasperation, and the bellicose conflict of egos and rapacities with salutary fertility, and in making love, faith, disinterestedness, and abnegation harmful. A distressing doctrine whose truth should be deplored as it is taught, but which, proven false, must be radically extirpated, because it is an encouragement of the evil it praises, and because it paralyzes the generous impulses rendered impotent by it.

It is possible to measure once again, just as for the question of fair price, the efficiency of a sociology which always follows the material path covered by ideas: in order to "unleash ferocious coveting" and to commit "assaults against the weak or the defeated," there must be a "doctrine"—and thus researchers, thinkers, media, and metrological chains. A doctrine that is all the more "distressing" as it does not settle—as the usual critics of natural selection do—for bringing humans down to the level of animals, but rather, and what is perhaps worse in Tarde's view, it brings the animal and the living down as well, to the level of what economism had tried to do with humans.

If there is one thing that Tarde will not allow, it is to justify war and the survival of the fittest: this refusal applies to plants and animals, as well as to men. This does not mean that conflicts did not exist. On the contrary, they make up half of the book. Never does he give himself over to the pleasures of a harmonious ecology which would appeal to the great peace of nature in order to be rid of human baseness. Conflicts are everywhere, but nothing guides them; there is no optimum which guarantees the survival of the fittest. There is no dialectic, there is no more Providence than there is Mephistopheles, no more God than there is the Devil. For Tarde, to naturalize does not mean to lower but on the contrary to *elevate* economic activity to the level of proliferation, multiplication, and invention, which will make it possible to explain the *content* of goods and not only the *form* of the exchange.

Redistributing Production Factors

Indeed, this Darwinian (but neither social nor neo-Darwinian) manner of conceiving of the intertwining of an economics of nature, makes Tarde, in a sense, an attentive observer of what was not yet, at his time, called biotechnology and bio-politics. Nothing prevents human beings from adding ends to these natures, now in the plural, that have no finality, given that they are all inventions from below, so to speak!

> The ideal end towards which humanity moves, without yet having a precise awareness of it, is, on the one hand, to compose, using the best of all of the planet's flora and fauna, a harmonious concert of living beings, working together, within a common system of ends, towards the very same ends as those of man, freely pursued; and, in addition, to capture all the forces, all the inorganic substances, to subjugate them, together, as simple means, to the now converging and consonant ends of life. It is from the viewpoint of this distant outcome that one must stand to understand the extent to which the fundamental conceptions of political economy need to be revised.

This is the revision that Tarde takes upon himself in his *Psychologie Économique*. By plunging economic activity back into the universal flow of monads, he never believes that it is possible to understand the inventions of economics as anything other than the *amplification* of the inventions of nature. What, in his view, is the principle production factor? The connecting of human inventions to the countless inventions of this nature, which nothing unifies.

> Is this only the reproduction of wealth? That could be, but on condition that we carry out a thorough analysis of this reproduction. To distinguish *land, capital and labor*, does not elucidate much for us. If we get to the bottom of these things we find that they work themselves out through different kinds of repetitions. What is *land* if not the ensemble of physical/chemical and living forces which act on each other and through each other, and some of which—heat, light, electricity, chemical compounds and substances—consist in radiating repetitions of ethereal or molecular vibrations, and the others, cultivated plants and domestic animals—in no less radiating and expansive repetitions of generations conforming to the same organic type or to a new race created by the art of gardeners and breeders?

We can see how Tarde solves the problem of naturalization: by coming nearer to the innovations, repetitions, and adaptations of things themselves, by offering them, as he says, new *habits*. The consequence that follows—so astonishing for today's reader, who is so quick to look for the factors of production in capital and work—is to see both of them redistributed.

> What is *labor*, if not an ensemble of human activities doomed to repeat indefinitely a certain series of learned acts, taught through apprenticeship, for example, whose contagion tends also to radiate ceaselessly?—And what

is *capital* itself, if not, in what, in my view, is its essence, a certain group of given inventions, but ones viewed by the person exploiting them as known, that is as though they had been transmitted to him by the inventors through an increasingly generalized and popularized intellectual repetition?

It seems that Tarde likes research but not work! He sings the praises, in 1902, of a civilization of leisure, cafes, conversation, fashion, trinkets, tourism. At the very moment when the iron law of ennui and mechanization was being imposed, when there would soon be the law of the division of labor, Tarde sings the praises of idleness, of the chatter of the idle classes, like in the following striking passage on one of his favorite hobby-horses: conversation as an essential production factor.

Conversation is eminently interesting to the economist. There is no economic relationship between men that is not first accompanied by an exchange of words, whether verbal, written, printed, telegraphed, or telephoned. Even when a traveler exchanges products with islanders whose language he does not know, these swaps only take place through the means of signs and gestures which are a silent form of language. In addition, how do these needs for production and consumption—for sale and purchase —which have just been mutually satisfied by a trade concluded thanks to conversation arise? Most often, thanks again to conversations, which had spread the idea of a new product to buy or to produce from one interlocutor to another, and, along with this idea, had spread trust in the qualities of the product or in its forthcoming output, and, finally, the desire to consume it or to manufacture it. If the public never conversed, the spreading of merchandise would almost always be a waste of time, and the hundred thousand advertising trumpets would sound in vain. If, for just one week, conversation ceased in Paris, it would show very quickly through the singular decrease in the number of sales in stores. There is no manager more powerful than consumption, nor, as a result, any factor more powerful—albeit indirect—in production than the chatter of individuals in their idle hours.

Marx would have not liked this argument. Sure, but what would today's viral marketing specialists say—those who calculate, with extremely sensitive mechanisms, the slightest mood variations on the most narcissistic of blogs? Here again, Tarde did not, in his time, possess the means to prove that the quantifications to which he aspired were possible, but today's general digitization makes it possible now to come back to his initial hypotheses, perhaps more profitably.

Capital Trends

A shocking reversal of values, inverting the harsh realities of material infrastructures? Tarde does not, in fact, reverse anything, because, for him, there is no infrastructure nor any superstructure. For he previously redistributed the factors of production, seeing, in the subtle variations of belief and desire, the true sources of value. While barely exaggerating, one can say that in economics, all is superficial, all is moral, all is irrational, all is subtlety. We have but to read Tarde's discussion of capital to be convinced:

In my view, there are two elements to be distinguished in the notion of capital: first, essential, necessary capital:

that is, all of the ruling inventions, the primary sources of all current wealth; second, auxiliary, more or less useful capital: the products which, born from these inventions, help, through the means of these new services, to create other products.

These two elements are different in more or less the same way as, in a plant seed, the germ is different from those little supplies of nutrients which envelope it and which we call cotyledons. Cotyledons are not indispensable; there are plants that reproduce without them. They are just very useful. The difficulty is not in noticing them, when the seed is opened, for they are relatively large. The tiny germ is hidden by them. The economists who saw capital as consisting solely in the saving and accumulation of earlier products are like botanists who would view a seed as being entirely made up of cotyledons.

"Cotyledon capital"! We can just imagine Lenin, in Zurich, reading Tarde and laughing uproariously at this ridiculous botanic and bucolic image. How far this is from the image of giant power hammers, from the smoking factories, from the workshops, from the strikes, and from the barricades which, at the time, ignited the spirit of the revolutionaries. But wait! Wait! The story is not yet finished. Those who today pass in front of the rusted remains of industrial ruins or who place flowers in front of the monuments erected in honor of the victims of revolutions ought to read with greater attention what differentiates, according to Tarde, "auxiliary capital" from "essential capital."

In short, the only thing that is absolutely indispensable for the production of a new engine is the detailed knowledge of an engine's parts, of how to manufacture them and, even before that, how to extract the materials from which they are made. This bundle of ideas, each of which is a large or small invention, owed to a known or unknown inventor, this bundle of inventions all gathered in a brain: that is the only portion of old products—for this is indeed a mental product, the fruit of school teaching—that is imperatively required for the building of an engine. And the same could be said for the production of any item.

Of course, the individual who, reduced to this intellectual legacy of the past, would have neither seeds, nor supplies, nor tools, would therefore be in a deplorable condition to carry out agricultural or industrial work. But it would not be impossible for him to produce, a bit sooner or a bit later—whereas, if, provided with the seeds or the most abundant materials, amassed and accumulated through savings, and with the most perfected equipment, he is at the same time ignorant of the secrets of the industry he claims to lead, or the methods of the culture in which he engages, he will be struck by production impotence in spite of all of his supposed capital.

We who find ourselves grappling, a century after this work, with so-called "knowledge societies," facing globalization, confronted with burning questions of technical research, politics, innovation, and who begin to penetrate into the most intimate abilities of living organisms, understand that the image of capital itself must change from top to bottom. To be sure, Tarde sometimes hesitates on the exact characterization of germ-capital. But, what interests him each time is the ability of germ-capital to vary over time, to differ.

Let us reflect for a moment on the different oppositions Tarde sets up to define the germinal character of capital. First of all, he redefines the distinction between capital and labor: "The distinction between capital and labor thus comes back, in essence, to that of a model and its copy." Let us try to see more clearly into this distinction which seems so odd to us, given that we are so used to thinking of labor as the main source of value.

If capital is the model and labor its copy, it is first of all because Tarde understands work in its most basic sense, in order to clearly detach what falls into the category of repetition from what falls into that of invention. Work is a raw force, an inertia without specific qualities and incapable of effecting differences in its own movement. Any change affecting it comes from the outside. Thus, the work of invention praised by labor sociologists as a trademark of the irreducibility of the human is already of a different order: it already contains myriad operators of differentiation that mold this raw force to its environment and adjust it so as to maintain its habits. Even the most repetitive labor, we know, requires a continuous production of small innovations that circulate and that are, in fact, small, preliminary resolutions of opposition. Labor alone can never diverge and effect differences in adversity: alone, it can only repeat and exhaust itself. Equipped with a model, it bends and lengthens its trajectory in order to get around obstacles. Tarde has the audacity to not take the work of invention—which is to say the stock in trade of labor sociologists—for a pure trend but rather to see in it a web and an intertwining of a raw force with active models mobilized according to oppositions. He pays very close attention to these models.

> [...] If he does not have any tools, the worker in the fields will manufacture them using simpler tools, or even using his fingers; deprived of colours or brushes, the painter will also manage to make them; but on one condition, which

is the only necessary one: that both worker and painter will have already seen tools and their making, which they will take as models, unless, having never seen them, or never seen them being made, they invent them.

Labor as raw force, then, strongly resembles "cotyledon capital"—secondary capital. These two species share the characteristic of not being able to deflect their trajectory autonomously. What is the reason for their lack of autonomy? Paradoxically, it is because they are trends which are *too pure*, which means that they are incapable of changing course. *Autonomy comes only to compounds*, only to those entities which are the results of unstable interferences. When the raw force of bare work consists of an example of a previous solution to a similar opposition, a difference can be effected. When inert matter finds itself plugged into a production technique, a process of *animation* is carried out, which brings us into the work of capital in the strict sense. Just like raw labor, cotyledon capital is an exercise in thought, a borderline case that is indeed difficult to find in the field of economic anthropology. In practice, it is always a compound which is encountered. But it is once again Tarde's analytical strength to point to the large conceptual trends that the notion of capital—and, as we shall see, that of capitalism—too quickly conflate.

In difficult but illuminating passages, Tarde comes to liken individuation, oscillation and germination. To be a genius and to be a germ are often confused. It is as much a redefinition of a germ as oscillation as it is a redefinition of genius as the intersection of lines of influence and imitation. Tarde even, at times, identifies the spirit with the germ, such as when he uses the expression "human capital," with the innovative ability of entrepreneurs in mind. But against an econo-mistic reading of human capital, whose posterity in the Chicago School in the person of Gary Becker we well know, Tarde places the line dividing the waters else-where. Once again the economic agent is not the only place for differentiation of the germ. One can even say that the *Homo economicus* is the poorest case of differen-tiation: faithful to his maximization maxims, he will be content with ratiocinating and repeating rather than differing. If one wants to find in economic literature an example of the work of germination, it is to John Maynard Keynes or Joseph Schumpeter that one should look, in the portraits they paint of entrepreneurs. There is thus a double reading of this new theory of capital brought by the germ. On the one hand, we have capi-tal as a source of oscillation, following Tarde's interest in *hesitation* (found in a number of his earlier writings). It is literally, using an expression which has become standard among the historians and sociologists of the contemporary sciences, a study of capital *in the making*.

But there is another possible reading of the germ-capital which minimizes its collaborative origin and its revolutionary dimension. Such a reading emphasizes instead the germ as a finished product that can be preserved and passed from one generation to another. The *potential* character of the germ is thus lost. Instead, what comes to the forefront is the close rela-tionship between the germinal form of capital and the memory capacity of the economic organizations that carry it.

A discovery or an invention, that might increase man's knowledge of power, or both at the same time, always manifests itself either within us, in the memory of our nerves or muscles, as a mental cliché, an acquired habit, a notion, a talent—or, on the outside, in a book or a machine. A book is but an extension and an appendix of our brain; a machine is an additional limb. We might say either that a book is an exterior memory or that a memory is an internal book, one that a sort of invisible librarian, hidden in our inner self, placed before our eyes at the desired moment. Similarly, a machine is an exterior talent and a talent is an inner machine.... Thus, the different and multiple skills of the craftsmen of old, their long apprenticeships and their gradual storing up of particular habits, all this was made largely useless by the construction of later machines. The latter are nothing more than the outward projection, as well as the often prodigious amplification of these talents and of the organs through which such talents are exhibited. And one can just as well say that, if the destruction of such machines forced talents to be revived, if, for example, the elimination of printing presses brought back calligraphers and manuscript illuminators, or if the elimination of textile mills brought back the old spinners, these reborn talents would be like the simplified and reduced re-embodiments of the destroyed machines.

Tools and memories are thus inextricably linked. The profound and the superficial, the internal and the external, the natural and the artificial—no category escapes the Tardian re-reading.

In redefining germ—or necessary—capital, Tarde also redefines cotyledon—or secondary—capital. It is not very difficult to be more precise on this topic than the economists, so slipshod was the manner in which the latter dealt with material capital, seen as a great heap of *undifferentiated* junk. Tarde's innovative thinking is nowhere more evident than in his crossed reading of the worlds of nature and artifice. Searching for what characterizes the tool, he comes to define it as a *gradient of resistance*.

> All tools, both those used for manual tasks and those used for intellectual tasks themselves, are, it should be noted, substances in the solid state, and not in the liquid or gaseous state.... Why is this the case? Because, you can only lean on something that puts up some resistance: solidity is both resistance and support. Equipment and solidity are two ideas so intimately connected that, even in animal and plant life, from one end to the other of the zoological scale, we can observe this indissoluble link. The tools of living creatures are the appendices or extensions of each cell. They are more or less mobile and always made out of a more or less resistant fabric, and they are the limbs of the organism as a whole, limbs that always have a certain solidity in relation to the rest of the body.

We see the tension between the germ and the cotyledon better after this mention of the essential solidity of tools and of physical capital. By distinguishing the destinies of the two forms of capital—the indispensable one which never stops inventing and differing, and the secondary one which always remains anchored to its habits—Tarde makes it possible to draw attention to a new range of variations: while germ capital always meets invention (or adaptation), cotyledon capital draws opposition to itself. The germ survives only by its versatility and its ability not to be frozen in a static formula but rather to explore new connections—and to avoid opposition by constantly adapting. Fixed capital, material capital, is never so lucky; it attracts opposition like a lightning rod.

An Economics of Compossibilities

Tarde endows infra-human or supra-human agencies with desires by once again breaking down the boundaries established by an economic theory more concerned with order than with the intelligibility of the associations between people and goods. His masterly example of the economics of books clearly illustrates the tension which runs through this new theory of capital. Tarde describes the book-as-asset as that which becomes capable of creating friends and enemies, attractions and repulsions, through a game of quotations and references.

> But, whether considered as product or as a teaching, a book is capable of allying itself with other books or of combatting them. There is no book, considered as a teaching, which is not made with other books, often given in the bibliography, and among which there are some of which one can say that it is made for them, because it confirms and completes them... If we were looking for the general conditions of the production of books, as economists have looked for those of the production of commodities, we would see that the famous distinction between the three factors of land, capital and labor can possibly be applied here but with some great and instructive transformations, particularly regarding capital, which should be construed as the ceaselessly growing bequest of worthy ideas from the past, of subsequent discoveries and inventions.

By its power in defining networks and in putting together aggregates, the book participates in the work of the germ. It can be drafted in an innovative series when it is made a precursor, an initiator of some novelty. It can also be rediscovered after several decades of slumber and reopen a whole continent for future research (much like Tarde's work!). When it is forgotten, it is but a repetitive specimen and a case of cotyledon-capital. But when it is rediscovered, its activity picks up again, just like bacteria that has been quiescent at low temperature. Once again, one must be careful not to be misled by the metaphor of the germ—code—and of the cotyledon—shapeless matter. Nothing is shapeless in Tarde's ontology, let alone in his economics. It is no coincidence that Tarde is Leibnizian: in each fish, there are ponds filled with more fish, and so forth, *ad infinitum*.

It is striking to note how Tarde's sharp attention to the circulation of examples and the processes of diffusion was present in the economic literature of the 1980s under the notions of standardization and path dependency. Such literature brought back to the forefront the specific material quality of economic goods themselves. The characteristics of these goods, which had been held at a distance and which entered into models as mere points in a continuous space (and thus points which could be moved about because they were, essentially, interchangeable), arise again as the sources of large-scale industrial deployment. Without always formulating them in the same way, these more recent economic theories take up the most original Tardian intuitions: not to assign a source to the economy (rarity, maximization, interest), but rather to assign it a psychology based on compatibility and harmony, on opposition and rhythms. Economics no longer rests on a pedestal or on an ultimate foundation site, but rather solely on the stability of a configuration. From this point of view, the divisions of traditional economic theory no longer make sense. Micro and Macro are but two arbitrary points which hide all the work of formatting, coordination, standardization and compatibility, and end up temporarily resolving certain conflicts through new adaptations.

There Has Never Been a "Capitalist Regime"

If we accept all of Tarde's strange ideas on production factors, we may notice that, decidedly, in our history, something other than the rise of capitalism has occurred. Tarde does not believe that any great split, radical revolution, or epistemological break occurred to upset economic history and give birth to the capitalist hydra.

> What really accumulates, as we know, because of a need that is not historical nor confined to our modern society, but rather logical and universal, is the germ-capital, that legacy of the indestructible ideas of man's genius. From this point of view, to speak of a *capitalist regime*, as if capitalism were a transitory phase of social development, would be to use the most ill-suited expression, the most likely to lead the spirit astray. When it comes to material-capital, born of this intellectual capital, it continuously self-destructs and reproduces itself, and it is to this alone that John Stuart Mill's remark concerning the speed with which capital regenerates itself after the ravages of war or revolution applies. But it does not always regenerate. We have seen it annihilated, never to rise again; and the spectacle of nations in decline, gradually growing poorer, is such as to convince us that there is no internal need forcing it always to grow.

What, then, happened under the name of capitalism? No "internal necessity" can explain it. Throughout *Psychologie Économique*, Tarde emphasizes another phenomenon, without any break with the past, which he defines as the *extension* or *intensification* of the networks of imitation and contamination with its resulting *mathematization*, which we must no longer confuse, as should by now be clear, with cool objectification. Never do we move from the old-fashioned charm of exchange to commercial abstraction. For Tarde, therefore, there is no rise in abstraction, no commodity fetishism, nor any decrease of passions or increase in coldness. We move from the past to the present through a greater intertwining of distances, through a greater interlacing, through a more intricate involvement of the new techniques in innovation, production, commercialization and communication. This is true, for example, for the passage from town criers to modern advertising:

> The reason behind this evolution, this gradual replacement of acoustic advertising by visual advertising, is that the latter is far more likely than the former to spread more widely. Its reach, through newspaper announcements, through the many examples of wall posters, can spread endlessly, whereas it is difficult and costly to greatly increase the number of town criers. Advertising, in short, evolves in the direction of greater and greater reach, free and easy. The number of acoustic advertisements would not be able to go beyond a certain number in the city streets without resulting in a general deafening, whereas the number of visual advertisements can grow without any one of them losing its distinct visual character, although they might become blurred in one's memory.

Here again we find the link noted earlier, between techniques and accounting instruments, on the one hand, and what we might call the *lengthening of networks*. Capitalism, as we shall see in the last section, indeed poses an immense political and moral problem which fascinates Tarde, but he does not cut into a historical anthropology through the sudden eruption of modernity and abstraction. Well before Fernand Braudel and Immanuel Wallerstein, it is in terms of networks and of the broadening of trust systems that one should grasp the anthropology of markets on the path to globalization. Their range can be extended, but they cannot be made less social, less inter-subjective, less passionately interested. One can "economize" a society, but one can neither rationalize it nor modernize it. So true is this that Tarde described even the Stock Market and its astonishing discoveries as familiar places, in the vein of traditional markets, or, rather, as places offering, *down to the very instruments*, the same inter-subjectivity, even more entangled, even more intense.

> I challenge anyone to justify, through reason alone, through the cold and judicious calculation of probabilities, for the use of sensible wits, left to their own devices, *without the influence of others*, the vaguely rhythmic oscillations of any given value, for example of the English stock over the last two centuries.

If you would like to understand why the economy is first and foremost inter-subjective, you have to head to the stock markets! There, you will not find abstraction, but, on the contrary, blinding evidence that all speculation there is a question, precisely, of speculation—in the inter-subjective and psychological sense of the duels discussed earlier. No one who tries to make sense of the recent world financial crisis will deny that Tarde must be right. Whereas the usual complaint is that finance has made the economy too abstract, however, on the stock exchange the economy works not on its head, but indeed on its feet.

> Before the broadening of the markets and the institution of Stock Exchanges, there were no forward sales to tyrannically fix the price of wheat. But was the price of wheat, under the Ancien Regime for example, determined by the real insufficiency or overabundance of wheat in a given region, or at a given time? No. At that time, when people were very ill-informed, when one knew only the harvest of one's one village, abundance or scarcity was judged based on the amount of wheat brought into the market hall of the little neighboring town. It was enough for a few monopolizers (for there were indeed such people then, just as today there are big bankers who play on the Stock Markets), to drain the harvests of one or two towns, or to stock their own harvest (in the case of large landowners), to create the appearance of an entirely artificial scarcity, which resulted nonetheless, as if it had been real, in a prodigious hike in the price of wheat.

We can see how far we are here from the idea of an *embeddedness* of the economic in the social. And this is for a critical reason to which Tarde dedicates many pages: through the spread of valuemeters, the economic discipline modifies the *calculability* of the social itself. Economics does not lower the temperature and the subjectivity of passions: through measure, it offers them a slight additional predictability. If the theory of the Stock Market is, for Tarde, just as important as the question of price formation, it is because in it, we can clearly see the entirely psychological passage *from uncertainty to probability*, a passage just facilitated, amplified, simplified, and formatted, by the spread of accounting instruments and calculating devices. Hence, the parallel between the history of the mathematization, economization and "financialization" of the social world, moving little by little, thanks to the proliferation of valuemeters, from one regime of uncertainty to another:

> Mathematical evolution moves from arithmetic to algebra, from the theory of numbers to that of functions. Monetary evolution moves from metal coins to paper money (a kind of *algebraic* sign of currency), and from the trade of commodity (where an amount of money is traded for an item or a service) to the trade of stock market values (where financial securities are exchanged for each other). On the stock market, values, which are relationships between sums of money and objects, are themselves *assessed* in relation to each other. It is a second-degree relationship. Through the quoted value, they present themselves as functions of each other, rising or falling together following certain laws.

That is why he can write the following sentence which essentially summarizes his whole book: "The tendency to *mathematize* economic science and the tendency to *psychologize* it, far from being irreconcilable, must thus instead lend each other mutual support in our view."

We are now in a position to understand how Tarde, setting aside all the usual divisions of treatises, will now divide the subject of his economic psychology.

> Instead of "production of riches" let us say *economic repetition*: by this we will understand the relations that

men entertain with one another, from the standpoint of the propagation of their similar needs, of their similar labors, of their similar judgments bearing on the greater or lesser utility of these labors and of their outcomes, or of their similar transactions...

Under the heading of economic opposition, I aim to understand the relations between men from the standpoint of the unnoticed psychological contradiction between their needs and their judgments of utility, from the standpoint of the more apparent conflict between their labors by way of competition, strikes, trade wars, and so on. The entire theory of prices, of cost-value, which presupposes internal struggles and the sacrifices of some desires to others, is also connected to this subject. Under the heading of economic adaptation, I will treat the relations that men entertain with one another from the standpoint of the cooperation of their old inventions to the satisfaction of a new need or the better satisfaction of an old need, or of the cooperation of their efforts and their labors in view of the reproduction of already invented riches (implicit or explicit association, natural or artificial organization of work.

Having undergone this transformation, economics will no longer be that "erratic block" which he mocked earlier:

If one agrees to attempt a recasting of political economy following this new model, one will see, I believe, what it can gain by eliminating what is foreign to it, by a better distribution of what belongs to it and which it already possesses, by acquiring what it had neglected to claim as its own. It will become both more clear-cut and denser, better delimited and better fulfilled. And at the same time, the fecundity of the tripartite classification that can be equally applied to the theory of knowledge, the theory of power, rights and duties, and to the aesthetics, will become apparent.

PART III
Economics Without Providence

The reader is now ready, we hope, to register the strangeness of a book which will allow him to gain a new grasp on economics—a raw, not a cooked one. He will above all have to get used to following trajectories that are not led by anything, that are not guided by any underlying structure, nothing that can be captured in advance by a law outside the phenomena it governs—especially not that of nature. By becoming Darwinian, genuinely Darwinian, nature in the hands of Tarde has, one might say, *lost its hand*, this *visible or invisible* hand which had animated it until then. All of Tarde's sociology, all of his metaphysics, rises up against what seems to be an ineradicable prejudice whenever it comes to economic questions: that there exists somewhere, in the market, in nature, in the State, a harmonization mechanism which we could rely on so as not to have to practice politics anymore. For Tarde, though, there is no Providence; that is the heart of the book, the knot towards which everything converges. As a result, we must make do otherwise than by trusting in the economics of economists, whether they be right-wing or left-wing. How can we do this? Necessarily through artifice and invention.

The Return of Politics in Political Economy

We find the argument in its clearest form both at the beginning and the end of the book. Let us begin with the end, with this declaration that we can call constructivist, *avant la lettre*.

> The entire political economy of Adam Smith and his school is based on the premise of the spontaneous agreement between egoisms: hence the economic harmonies of Bastiat. The question is to know if these personal interests achieve harmony on their own or artificially. This question cuts the opposite way from that of Smith, for anyone who embraced economic opposition in its entirety, which showed us the hostility of interests, which is so frequent, and so often essential and radical. It follows that the harmonization of interests can only be obtained through artifice, and inventions are this artifice.

Let us remember that this is written in 1902, twelve years before the cataclysm of the Great War which will leave us stunned for a century, fifteen years before the Russian Revolution, right in the middle of the debate between liberalism and socialism, laissez-faire and protectionism—a debate still current in the form of "neo-liberalism" and "anti-globalization." Tarde, because he renewed social theory in his other books as much as the ties between the social and natural sciences, can finally ask the mother of all questions, in terms of "artifice" and "invention": it is the return of the word "political" in the phrase "political economy," an obviously impossible return as long as people believed in the existence of a material infrastructure governed by "natural laws" smuggled in from a biology of fantasy.

> The distinction between Politics and Political Economy, thus understood, is as clear cut as possible. One looks for the path towards the strongest collaboration among the desires of a nation or of a party in one same endeavor; the other looks for the path of their greatest and most reciprocal usage—two very different ways of understanding their adaptation.

There is no more an "embeddedness" of the economic in the social (for the good reason that the social is not a domain on its own, but a principle of association and contamination) than there is a political realm which would limit, along a border to be defined, the empire of what is economic. There is no domain at all: there is only an expanding fabric of interweaving desires and beliefs, each of which benefits more or less greatly from the techniques of communication—from the newspaper to the telegraph, all the way to the chatter of the idle classes—as well as from calculating devices—from the prices on price-tags all the way to the Stock Exchange and the collection of statistical data. Put otherwise, *economics and politics deal with the same object*, follow the same fabric, feel their way around the same networks, depend on the same influences and the same contaminations.

How can we distinguish them then? Only by the type of organization they promote: "collaboration" for politicians; "reciprocal use" for economists. We can indeed speak of harmonization concerning them, but this is not given by a law of evolution: it is a problem whose solution depends on our own inventions.

> Finally, in order for production to best adjust itself to consumption, is it not necessary for each of these terms to harmonize as best as possible with itself, that is, for the different types of production to hamper each other as little as possible, to help each other as much as possible, to converge as much as possible towards common national goals? For there to be, in short, the best possible organization, whether spontaneous or conscious, of work; and for the different kinds of needs and consumptions to conform, in their spontaneous or conscious hierarchy, to the most logical possible sort of common plan of conduct and of general life? These are two major problems which have plagued societies since the beginning of time and which have been given a series of solutions. Concerning the first, there was the *slave* solution in Antiquity, the *monastic* and *guild* solution in the Middle Ages, the *liberal* solution of current times, as we wait for the *socialist* solution or any other one, whose formula is being sought.

It is useless to dream of a development of economics such that politics would no longer be necessary; it is useless to dream of a development of politics such that economics would no longer need to play out. There are only different ways of organizing and dividing up passionate interests. In the intertwining of desires and beliefs, everything has to be the object of an artificial organization. We cannot leave it in anyone's hands. There may be a "life plan," a "common plan of conduct"; only one thing is certain: they will be immanent, contingent, and orchestrated, not transcendent. But in order to grasp the power of this constraint, of this immanence, we have to get to the bottom of this question of Providence, all the way to the ultimate source of the doctrine of *intelligent design*.

The "Adam Smith Problem" and the Question of God

How to find the "artifices" whose discovery will henceforth occupy political life, without being able to rely on a natural science? How to become inventive in political economy as well? The same question is posed at the beginning of the book when, over several astonishing pages, written years before the approaches of Schumpeter and Albert Hirschmann, Tarde discusses what is commonly called the "Adam Smith problem" and gives it, as he so often does, an entirely original solution. The problem is well-known: how can we explain that the author of *The Wealth of Nations* is also the author of the *Theory of Moral Sentiments* when Smith himself never drew a connection between the two works? "One could say that an almost airtight wall separates, within him, his two orders of research." Tarde, like all economic historians, is surprised by this.

What is nonetheless surprising is the small role played by psychology in these economic writings of Smith and the total absence of *collective psychology*. It is he, though, Smith himself, who was the first to study *sympathy*, a source and foundation of inter-mental psychology. How is it that he never felt the need nor the opportunity to make use of the keen observations he had made concerning the mutual stimulation of sensibilities, in order to explain the economic relationships of men?

Who, then, is this absent one, this Great Other, whose presence Smith does not even need to mention, so obvious it is to him? Tarde's answer is a theological one:

We can understand that a man so willing to see a divine artist behind the canvas of human events and a divine wisdom behind all human folly, must have had no difficulty in seeing egoism itself, the love of the self, as vested with a sacred function, one that is eminently suited to weave and strengthen social harmony. Thus, when he based all of political economy on that principle, and reduced *homo economicus* to interest, of course setting aside all affection and all abnegation, it was not, for him, the effect of an epicurean and materialistic conception. It was, on the contrary, a natural continuation of his piety and his faith in God. Behind the egoistic man, there was a beneficent God, and the apology of the former's egoism was, in truth, but a hymn in prose to the infinite goodness of the latter.

To the "invisible procession" of which he spoke earlier, we must add God. Now this is economic anthropology, and of the deepest kind. But it is an anthropology that can be practiced only on condition that the link between the assessments of the human heart and the calculations that allow for the wealth of nations be renovated. Egoism is sacred; it is viewed as sacred. Take away God, and everything collapses!

> But Smith's successors, in our century, are athe-
> ists.... Or, at the very least, if they do believe in God, their
> speculations carry no trace of this belief. That is why, by
> continuing to base political economy on the premise of
> man's pure egoism and the battle of interests, after having
> banished the idea of Providence, they eliminated, without
> realizing it, the keystone of the system, which has lost all
> of its former solidity. They have, if we prefer, eliminated
> heaven from this now incomprehensible landscape, or
> put out the light of the lantern, which no longer illuminates
> or explains anything.

The "keystone" of the economic "system" is God! Let us not misunderstand Tarde's intentions. Unlike so many truly reactionary thinkers of the 19th century, such as Joseph de Maistre or Louis de Bonald, Tarde does not in any way wish to argue that we should once again trust ourselves to the care of divine Providence! His point is far more ironic, he goes much deeper, his approach is much more biting towards all scientific pretensions: those atheist economists who came after Smith are only atheists for fun. They pretended to eliminate Smith's God, who had been in charge of regulating the relationship between economy and morality, all the while upholding the principles of a theocratic order. They settled for placing an airtight wall between the two orders of phenomena. The hand has perhaps become invisible, but it is still the hand of the All-Powerful, which alone can make us obey without grumbling against the laws of economics. The illusion runs deep, but what is most astonishing is that it has worked for two centuries, and never more than today has it been displayed: a God who is crossed out, negated, and denied, still regulates the automatic achievement of harmony.

What Tarde demands of economists is a bit of honesty: if you really want your optimum, your harmonies, your natural laws, your inflexible iron laws, to be religious and providential, then, for the love of God, say so! But do not act as though, behind this "secular religion," to use Polanyi's phrase, you had really secularized economics. In other words, economics is still searching for an approach that would be able to make it, finally, materialistic and atheistic. For Tarde, everything in modern economics is marked by the seal of transcendence and of the sacred. As Nietzsche wondered about science: "How we, too, are still pious?"

The Likely Mistake of the Coming Socialism

The objection may be raised that there existed, at the same period, several socialist schools that aimed, too, to reveal the exploitation that is hidden behind vain claims of objectivity, and, above all, to put politics back into economics—and to do so far more vigorously. But Tarde knows these doctrines well; he is passionate about the social question; he reads Marx with the same attention as he reads Darwin. Nevertheless, he does not treat the diffusion of Marx's doctrines any differently than he does the spreading of the ideas of Malthus or Spencer. At no time does he think that they will reveal the presence of indisputable facts behind the smokescreen of ideologies. There is nothing more foreign to Tarde than the notion of an ideology which could hide or invert true science. If Marxism spreads, it is through the same mechanisms as all other forms of imitative rays:

> If workers from the most diverse professions form coalitions, it is only with a view to the famous "class struggles." When such a coalition is produced, it is always through the initiative and rousing propaganda of the workers from a professional body that stands out and is specifically designated for this mission, such as that of typographers, and it is only after many elements of resistance, defeated one after the other by many personal influences and suggestions, that repeated assemblies result in this alliance both on the offensive and the defensive.

"Class struggles," just as the "pure and perfect market," do not form the basis of the economy, but rather one of the possible versions of the economic discipline. While, for the pure and perfect market, scholarly journals and papers are necessary, for class struggles, what is needed is "repeated assemblies" and "propaganda." As always, Tarde invites us not to jump immediately outside of the point-to-point networks which convince, link by link, individual by individual. That is what allows him to offer a both generous and yet unforgiving assessment of Marxism. Tarde gives Marx credit for having been innovative concerning the passions, but yet without having questioned the economists' inversion of the recto and the verso.

> The socialist schools, as well as the French schools of 1848 and the German schools of today, thawed political economy and made it passionate; and it is in this way alone that they introduced a new psychological element into it, which did not, by the way, change anything in the

fundamental notions. The passion that inspired these doctrines often varied; and, in the combination of generosity and hatred of which it is composed, the proportions of the two are reversed; while more generous than hateful in France, it has become more hateful than generous in Germany. Compare Leroux or Proudhon even to Karl Marx. Under the empire of these intense feelings, economic theories became more colorful and invigorated, but, at heart, they maintained and even accentuated the old claim of *objectivity*, of the geometrical deduction of rigid formulas, having the appearance of physical laws.

Marxists have not set aside from the old dialectic the Mephistophelian taste for war, the "mother of all things," and they have maintained the idea of a direction, structure, design and law in history. In essence, one transcendence has taken the place of another: *the gaining of passion is great, the gaining of immanence is none*. The God, the Mammon, the Devil of harmony is always venerated. Thus, in Tarde's view, Marxism offers the worst of both worlds: a growth of the passions and a growth of the claim of objectivity. In other words, thanks to him, we will begin to hate, in the name of science, on an even greater scale! Crimes committed in the name of dialectical materialism will be able to add themselves to the crimes justified by capitalism. In 1902? You must admit, that's not bad.

But let us note that there is nothing nostalgic about Tarde's argument, nor is there anything reactionary or simply defensive. He finds it fascinating that socialism was able to innovate on the very nature of economic *passions*. What he is concerned with is therefore not socialism in itself, of which he approves the general direction, but rather the difficulty in organizing production, both from a *technical* and a quasi-accounting point of view.

> The socialist standpoint on the organization of work can be considered as the fusion of the political and economic standpoints into one, through the absorption of the second by the first. The originality of socialism consist in having added, to the very small number of collective goals that men united in a nation can pursue—patriotic glory, war, conquest, defense of territory—a great new goal, very much worthy of their efforts: the conscious and systematic organization of work. Except that, were this goal to be attained, it would become far more difficult for a new need, and consequently, for a new industry, to interpose itself in the chain of recognized needs. Work will ossify itself by organizing itself.

The doubts that Tarde has about socialism and, in particular, its Marxist version, do not rest at all, we can see, on a sort of moral or political aversion. He skips over all of the objections with which his contemporaries concerned themselves. He gives socialism its chances, and designates with tact the central point of the whole theory: can the economy be rendered *predictable* by economics? Let us remember that, for Tarde, there is no infrastructure, no automatism, no harmony; there are no natural laws, no laws of development; everything rests on artifice and inventions, facilitated, coordinated, simplified, gathered and assembled by the measuring instruments which feed the economic discipline and which spread out from the metrological chains. It is only through the spreading of instruments that the social is rendered both quantifiable and predictable to itself, through a powerful process of reflexivity. Now, economics as a discipline, in making itself mathematical, can do a lot, but it can only format the economy which always overflows from it on all sides. "Future invention: that is the pitfall of all calculations; that is the unexpected against which all prophecies come up."

> The question [of the socialist organization of labor], is, in essence, to know whether we will ever be able, through marvelously rapid commercial statistics, both certain and perfect, and through other means of information, to render certain or almost certain the predictions, always more or less conjectural today, of producers, so that there might be no more risk run, nor, as a result, any more injustice or inconvenience in eliminating the boss's profit, a necessary compensation for his current risks. If the day came when nature and the extent of consumers' demands could be thus predicted with certainty by producers, then, and only then, would the State be able to think seriously about taking their place, directing from above centralized and organized national work, or, at the very least, workers would be able to lay claim to their part of the boss's profits, their boss having become their colleague, a more intelligent and talented colleague, and better paid as such and as the creator of the business, but not because of risks taken, given that such risks would no longer exist.

It makes us wonder what we accomplished in the 20th century, since the question essentially remains today with the same intensity as yesterday—or, rather, with even greater intensity, because passionate interests have grown and combined enormously. The question of risk-sharing, of what is good and what is bad, of State organization, of the quality of data, of the coordination of agreements between likes and dislikes, and, above all, of the predictability that can be given to the habits contracted by the swarming of attachments, that is indeed the substance of political economy. Yet, if Tarde doubts the ability of socialism to solve these questions, it is because he doubts the virtues of regimentation:

> In principle, then, there is nothing inconceivable about this. But, I must say, if I consult experience, that I do not see any less that there is very little basis for the dream of a general and centralized organization of work by the State. Never, without a doubt, will it be possible to predict the needs of all citizens with as much rigor and certainty as those of a marching army; nevertheless, we know how flawed even the most perfect military supply organization is in a time of combat. Not a day passes without either the excess or the shortage of required supplies making itself painfully felt. All the more, under the collectivist regime, we would have reason to complain daily of civilian supply systems, whose task would be complicated in a completely different way.

There is nothing messier than war; nothing messier than the economics of war; nothing messier than communism, which would take total mobilization as an ideal model for the economy. Of course, Tarde, like all those of his time, was terribly mistaken on the future of coordination and perpetual peace, which, in their view, the first great wave of globalization heralded. And yet, October 1917 would soon take on the task of verifying this prediction concerning what could be expected from the socialism of war. If there is one thing that totalitarianism is incapable of following through with, it is *totalization*.

CONCLUSION

If You Chase the Big Beast Away, It Comes Galloping Back

It is decidedly not easy to be agnostic when it comes to economics. Neither Smith, nor the inventors of the market, nor socialism have yet achieved it. As long as politics is not recognized as a "power of invention," to use Maurizio Lazzarato's title, there will not be any taking back of economics by politics, and thus no socialism. We have to go even further and recognize, behind the Market's invisible hand, behind the State's visible hand, the same barely secularized figure, the social Organism, the Big Animal. That is what we will need to tackle in order to truly get to the bottom of the subject of economics.

In order to understand what makes Tarde so innovative in economics, it is necessary to fully grasp the innovation he brings to sociology. The idea, made famous by Polanyi, of an "embeddedness" of that which is economic in that which is social had the great impracticality of assuming the prior existence of society. We can understand, then, that the theoretical gain could not be very great: in passing from economism to economic sociology, all that was happening was shifting an already-established structure—the infrastructure and its laws—to another structure, it, too, already in place: society and its laws. Of course, we learned a lot about the "extra-economic" factors of contracts, of trades and of tastes, but it was, in a way, to move from one structure to another. Yet, the "involution" Tarde proposes of all the laws of a structure in the swarming of monads had the drastic consequence of dissolving all structures—that of the pure and perfect market, of course, but *also* those of the social world which are accepted by sociologists like Durkheim and his disciples. Along with the dissolution of society, all the metaphors of embeddedness also disappear. Economics no longer lies in the Procustian "bed" of the social, because there is no more bed, no more pillow to rest one's head, no more canopy, no more duvet.

In a decisive passage, Tarde brings together all of his sociological, economic and political thought—it was the last course he taught at the Collège de France, two years before his death—by showing by which paradoxical link the idea of harmony through the market and the idea of society always, deep down, went hand-in-hand.

Thus, there is no social harmony, and especially no economic harmony not preceded and prepared by a psychological harmony, and at the origin of all associations between men we will find an association between a man's ideas. Let us pause for a moment to point out the philosophical significance of the fact just observed. It follows, of course, that society is not an organism; but does it follow that it is not a reality which is distinct from its members? Now here is a question which demands a clear answer. If the idea of a social organism can be defended, it is only insofar as it is an expression, albeit an unfortunate one, of social realism, that is to say of society seen as a real being and not just as a *certain number* of real beings.

Totus aut omnis? The question remains. From the beginning of his career, Tarde argues against those—Comte, Spencer, Durkheim—who wish to distinguish rigidly the type of reality that is Society from the types of realities of the "real beings" who make it up. Where all sociologists would like to see two orders of reality—the Macro and the Micro— Tarde insists, page after page, on proving that, precisely in the case of human societies grasped from within, we know without a doubt that there is only one order of reality. Never, from among the gathered associates, does the social structure, this *cosa mentale*, suddenly emerge.

And yet, as intimate, as harmonious as a given social group may be, one never observes springing up *ex abrupto* in the midst of surprised associates a common *self*, a real and not merely metaphorical self, the wonderful result of which they would be the conditions. Without a doubt, there is always an associate who represents and personifies the whole group, or else a small number of associates (the ministers of a State), each of whom, in a particular manner, represents no less fully an individual manifestation of it. But this leader or these leaders are always also members of the group, born of their own fathers and mothers and not of their subjects or collectively of those they manage.

Despite a century of passing over this *pons asinorum* of social theory again and again, it is clearly not a question here of opposing holism and individualism. As we have seen, for Tarde it is no more true that there is the individual than that there is society. It is necessary to find a solution other than "social realism" to the question of the composition of that which is social, since "social realism" is a most *unrealistic* solution, that we still continue, a century later, to draw from the alleged opposition between individual and society.

Yet, the best support for this conception, might that not be the discovery of the "natural laws" which, independent of any individual will, might lead individuals, along paths already traced, to a more and more perfect political, moral, and economic organization? The doctrine of laissez-faire thus has much in common with that of society-as-organism, and the blows directed against the latter have repercussions on the former. If we were right to believe in the spontaneous harmonization of societies, we would also be right to view society as a real being, as we do a plant or an animal. But, really, is the illusion of this providential predestination not dissipating more and more, even from an economic point of view? When it comes to the political point of view, it is enough to open one's eyes to see nations rising and falling, strengthening or weakening, according to whether or not they have found, at the right moment, the strong hand of a statesman; and it is no longer possible to believe in an innate sense of direction that guides peoples with no apparent driver.

On both sides of the battle of giants which pits interventionism against laissez-faire, socialism against neo-liberalism, there are the same principles of sociology (the idea of "organism"), the same economic principles ("providential predestination"), and the same ethical principles ("the belief in the spontaneous harmonization of societies"). But how else can it be done? How can one escape this "seductive mistake"?

> However, should renouncing this error [that of society-as-organism], so seductive for so long, lead us to deny all specific reality of the social whole, to view it as a simple total, a numerical expression of the assembled individuals? No. If we refuse to allow natural laws in the given sense, and also formulas for evolution which are their most recent form, we are allowing in every individual a more or less acute need for the logical coordination of ideas, for the final coordination of acts, a need which is kindled through the coming together of individuals, and which becomes a general trend toward a growing logic and finality, in any category of social facts, and ends up making order out of disorder everywhere, and carding chaos into a world.

"To card chaos into a world": that is the goal that we might offer to passionate interests. There is no harmony, there are no natural laws, no "evolutionary formulas" like those that dialectical materialism popularized at the time, no revolution to expect—but that does not mean that one should, through a pleasant expectation of postmodernism, abandon the ideas of totality and finality. There is indeed for Tarde a "social whole" but—and this is what distinguishes him from all of his contemporaries, indeed from all of *our* contemporaries, and what gives his book such a pristine novel character—this social whole is *to be built*, through inventions, through artifice. It is in front of us, not behind us. Finalism is not transcendent and external, but rather immanent and internal, simply "kindled" and made "more logical" by the very way individuals, their ideas and their passions come together and connect, on condition that they effectively "card chaos into a world." To become a world, in other words, is one possibility among others. There is nothing inevitable about it. As a result, it may *not* come about; it can fail. Chaos can dissolve it. And Tarde concludes this bit of bravura with a profession of faith:

> This manner is different from that of providential harmonies or linear evolutions in that, instead of forcing the social train to follow a single path, always the same one, it gives it far more freedom. And, from there, we are led not to deny social reality but to conceive of it as alive and real in an altogether different way, rich in manifestations and in unexpected itineraries in an altogether different way. An algebraic formula that provides solutions to a great number of different problems is one thing, an arithmetical equation that applies to one problem only and contains one solution only is something else. I am a realist as well, in the sense that only society brings to reality, in my view, like in the view of my opponents, potentialities contained within individuals and which each of them separately would not be able to bring to fruition; but I hold that these potentialities are individual ideas and wills, I situate them in the brains instead of placing them nowhere other than in ontological clouds; and I say that these potentialities are innumerable, inexhaustible, just like their spiritual source, instead of limiting them to a strictly determined or rather predetermined number.

We must understand that the expression "political economy" does not have the same meaning at all, depending on whether we unite or oppose two providences, that of Society and that of the Market, or on whether we deny *all* providences, that of Society as well as that of the Market, the care of ensuring our common existence in advance. For, in order to finally be "realistic," one would need to agree to inherit an entirely different history, one which does not follow a "linear evolution," one which would accept being freed from the "ontological clouds," and which would give the "social train" "free play." It might be objected that we are dealing here with a charming enthusiasm, one which does not commit us to anything. Let us note, however, that it is indeed economic science that Tarde means to renew, and that we must take the parallel he draws between the passing from determination to freedom and the passing from "arithmetic" to "algebra" extremely seriously. At no time does Tarde ask us to choose between cold economics and warm subjectivity. Instead, it is from the free play of passionate interests that he expects more quantification, which is to say more social connections, to "card chaos into a world." ∎

Also available from Prickly Paradigm Press:

continued